Scarborough

DAVI

GW00648270

Dalesman

Dalesman Publishing Company Ltd
Stable Courtyard, Broughton Hall,
Skipton, North Yorkshire BD23 3AZ
www.dalesman.co.uk

First Edition 2000

Text © David Jeffels
Illustrations © John Ives

Maps by Jeremy Ashcroft and Harry Salisbury

Cover: Scarborough's South Bay by Mike Kipling

A British Library Cataloguing in Publication record
is available for this book

ISBN 1 85568 175-7

Printed by Amadeus Press, Huddersfield

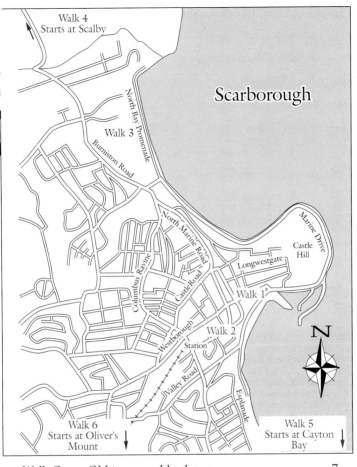

PUBLISHER'S NOTE

Introduction

Holidaymakers have been visiting Scarborough for over three centuries – all for the good of their health! Initially it was the gentry who went by horse and carriage to take the medicinal waters at the Spa but the opening of the railway marked a dramatic change in the town's fortunes enabling the working man to take his family to the seaside.

The town itself is over a thousand years old – it was founded by two Viking brothers, Kormak and Thorgils who established a stronghold. It was natural that it should be named after its founder, and as Thorgils was nicknamed Skarthi, the derivation of Scarborough's medieval name, Scardeborg from Skarthiburg seems obvious.

An ancient borough with records of Royal Charters from 1181, a famed port and fashionable Spa town, Scarborough today has a population of just under 50,000 and is one of Britain's most popular seaside resorts and a famous conference centre. Within its 5200 acres the town boasts 400 acres of parks and public gardens.

In recent years its economy has become more diverse with the changing pattern of holidaymaking. While tourism still accounts for much of its economy – it attracts some two and a half million visitors a year – the town also manufactures luxury holiday coaches, is a leading producer of frozen food and has a reputation for being one of the country's leading printing centres. Here thousands of holiday postcards, calendars and brochures for top international companies are produced.

Scarborough claims to be the cradle of Britain's tourist industry for it was here in the 1690s that the corporation of the day decided to sell the spa waters from a small wooden house.

A wonderful character by the name of Dickie Dickinson was appointed the first governor and in effect became the nation's first tourism director!

The writer of a letter in 1733, describing the bathing season at Scarborough, commented "It is the custom for not only gentleman but the ladies also, to bathe in the seas. The gentlemen go out a little way to sea in boats and jump in naked directly! The ladies have the conveniency of gowns. What virtues our physicians ascribe to cold baths in general are much more effectual by the additional weight of salt in sea-water – an advantage which no Spa in England can boast of but Scarborough. "

Over the centuries Scarborough has seen several military conflicts, not least the Civil War and more recently the town was the first to suffer during the German bombardment in 1914 which resulted in the famous First World War poster "Remember Scarborough", the original painting of which hangs in the town hall. It is therefore fitting that the motto on Scarborough's coat of arms is translated as "Let us rejoice thee to set dangers at nought in the quest of honour".

Situated between two magnificent bays, divided by a headland on which stands the remains of the 12th century castle, Scarborough has long-boasted of being 'The Queen of Watering Places' – a holiday resort which has something for everyone. I was persuaded to return to Scarborough, my home town, for a year. Thirty years on, and with the honour of Mayor of the Borough, behind me, I'm still here enjoying what I believe is one of the finest places in Europe.

I hope your stay is enhanced by experiencing some of these walks which show that there is more to Scarborough than its beaches and gardens.

Old town and harbour

Length of walk: 2 miles
Start/finish: Scarborough Town Hall

John A. Ins/00.

This walk includes many of Scarborough's historic features with the opportunity to see the harbour and its fishing fleet in action.

The **Town Hall**, originally a family mansion, replaced an early imposing house demolished in 1844. Its owner, John Woodall, was said to be so disillusioned that his panoramic views of the South Bay and The Spa had been spoiled by the construction of the Grand Hotel, that he decided to sell it.

By coincidence, the then Scarborough Corporation was looking for a new Town Hall and bought St Nicholas House, as it was then known, for £33,375 in a deal which included several other properties on the Foreshore and King Street.

The new Town Hall was opened in 1903 by Princess Henry of Battenberg who at the same time unveiled the statue in the gardens of her mother, Queen Victoria.

From the Town Hall turn left, and in doing so admire the imposing **Royal Hotel**, one of the oldest hotels in Britain and which has played host to many famous personalities, notably Sir Winston Churchill, nearly all post-war Prime Ministers, not to mention a bevy of show business stars.

In the days when Scarborough was able to accommodate the Conservative and Labour Party conferences, the Royal became the nerve centre of the Government of the day, with direct lines being set up to The White House and The Kremlin, enabling the day-to-day running of Government to continue for the Prime

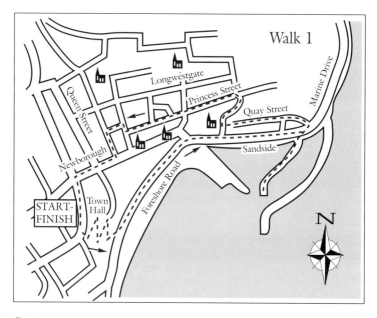

Fishermen's Offices

John A. Ives, '00

Minister, albeit from a seaside town on the Yorkshire Coast, rather than Westminster.

Just south of the Town Hall gardens is **King's Cliff**. Take this pathway which leads into St Nicholas Gardens and make your way leisurely down its pathways and steps from which you will take in spectacular views of the South Bay and seafront with the flashing lights of the amusement centres, cafes and ice cream parlours.

Sampling an ice cream – from any of the manufacturers who have been associated with Scarborough for generations – is a must. I guarantee your only complaint will be the generous size of the scoops!

As you head towards the harbour you will pass the **Lifeboat House** on your right where you can see the present boat. Climb the surrounding stairs to view the highly-sophisticated technology used to guide it in the most severe of weather and seas; study the records of the hundreds of rescues which the

Scarborough lifeboats have been involved in, and the lives its crews have saved, since the station – one of the oldest in Britain – was established in the 19th century.

Adjoining the station are to be found a row of kiosks selling seafood. Their superbly arranged displays of freshly caught crabs, lobsters, whelks, mussels are a must for all lovers of such delicacies.

The imposing red-brick building at the entrance to the West Pier has recently been restored to its former glory, providing offices and a nerve centre for several harbour businesses. Nearby is to be found The Ocean's Pantry where possibly the freshest fish in Britain is sold – directly off the market a few yards away!

Just a few paces on, and you find yourself on the **North Wharf** and the fishing fleet spread out across the harbour. It dates back to 1225 when Henry III provided 40 oaks from his woods to enable the original harbour to be built. Some 26 years later he granted a Royal Charter to the town's bailiffs and burgesses to build a new port of timber and stone.

Some 300 years later, Elizabeth I gave £500, plus 100 tons of timber and several tons of iron, to rebuild the harbour again, and there was a further Royal gesture in 1732 when George II approved the spending of £12,000 to enlarge it, making it one of the busiest ports in Britain with over 300 sailing ships.

Today, the harbour continues to thrive with a fleet which lands some of the finest fish in Britain, much of which finds its way into the country's top hotels. The growth in the leisure market has seen the harbour become an increasingly popular haven for yachtsmen, and now one of the main centres on the East Coast for surfers.

Walk around the North Wharf to the **Vincent Pier**, also known as the **Lighthouse Pier**, one of three piers in the harbour which has been protecting shipping for some 250 years. At the end of the pier you will find the **Lighthouse** which still plays a key role in guiding boats in and out of the harbour. The original, built in 1812, was so seriously damaged in the bombardment of Scarborough by German cruisers in 1914, that it had to be demolished and rebuilt.

Return to Sandside via the Vincent Pier, and on the right behind the complex of restaurants, shops and arcades, is to be found **Quay Street**, the oldest part of the town where the Vikings settled after they colonised Scarborough in 966. Remains of timber-framed buildings have been discovered by archaeologists over the years and digs are still undertaken today. Of particular interest is **The Three Mariners**, a cruck-framed house, now a private residence, which was a well-known smugglers' haunt in the 17th and 18th centuries. Turn right into Sandside to **The King Richard III House Restaurant,** a building dating back to 1350, one of the oldest surviving in Scarborough. The King stayed there when Duke of Gloucester. He used Scarborough as his headquarters because he also held the title of Admiral of the Yorkshire Coast. The house boasts quaint passageways and cupboards which may well have been used by those wanting to evade the customs men or press gangs.

As you wander along Quay Street towards The Bolts and Eastborough look out for such unusually named areas as Dog and Duck Lane, Bakehouse Steps, and Long Greece Steps. Just a few yards into Eastborough is East Sandgate. It is worth the short steep climb to find **The Buttercross**, opposite the Leeds Hotel in West Sandgate, tucked away behind railings on the left – the last surviving legacy of the legendary Scarborough Fair, made famous by pop stars Simon and Garfunkel in a song which is now performed by artistes and orchestras worldwide.

A few more paces on is Princess Square. From here walk straight ahead into St Sepulchre Street and to the **Market Hall**, in whose catacomb-type basement can be found a fascinating complex of craft stalls.

Leaving the Market Hall, and St Helen's Square, walk up Eastborough to St Nicholas Street where a few hundred yards on the left you will return to the Town Hall.

North Bay, castle and Peasholm

Length of Walk: Approx 2.5 miles
Start: St Mary's Parish Church; finish: town centre

Few towns can boast a parish church with such breathtaking views as Scarborough. **St Mary's** dates back to 1180 and originally belonged to the Abbey of Citeaux. Its history is closely linked with that of the town itself, having suffered extensive damage during the Civil War.

In 1198, Richard I granted the church to the Cistercians, but it was seized by Henry VI and granted to Bridlington Priory.

The west front of the church, formerly with two towers, is the earliest part of this beautiful old building. The surviving south transept was built in the 14th century and later in the century, the barrel-vaulted chapels were added to the south aisle and a second aisle built in the north.

The aisled chancel was rebuilt in the mid-15th century but was badly damaged in the siege of the nearby Norman Castle in 1644/5 and ruined by the fall of the central tower in 1659. The present tower was built in 1669 and the outer north aisle in the mid-19th century.

Its bells won awards at the Great Exhibition of 1851.

From the south door of St Mary's are to be found memorable views over the harbour, South Bay, and over to Flamborough

Head – a wonderful place to sit and absorb the atmosphere of hundreds of years of history.

Immediately north of the original churchyard, across the appropriately named lane, Paradise, is a detached burial ground where **Anne Brontë**, who died in 1849, is buried. She spent several holidays in Scarborough and died in a house on the site where the Grand Hotel now stands.

From the site of her grave, climb the old road to the **Castle** which has dominated Scarborough's skyline for over 800 years and survived many bloody battles.

The first castle was built by William le Gros, Earl of Albemarle, 70 years after Hardrada raided Scarborough in the 12th century. King John made several visits to the castle, Edward I held court there in 1275 and Richard III was a visitor in 1484.

In all, the castle underwent five sieges, in 1312, 1536, 1557, in 1644-5, and in 1648.

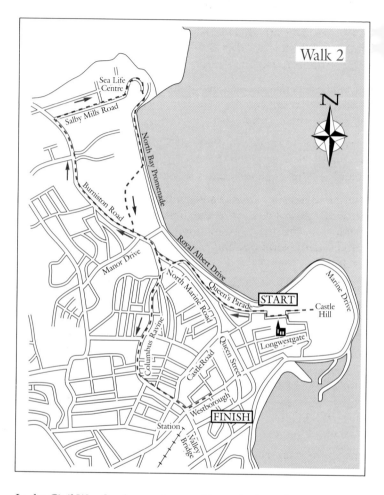

In the Civil War, Scarborough was ultimately the only Royalist port on the East Coast and it was not until 1645, with the garrison worn out and stores exhausted, that the castle surrendered to Parliament.

For more than a year in 1665-66, George Fox, the founder of The Society of Friends, was imprisoned in the ruined Charles' Tower of the castle. He suffered great hardships before he was released by order of Charles II.

In 1914 at the start of the First World War, the German fleet bombarded the town and castle. The keep was damaged and the 17th century barracks almost entirely destroyed.

In recent years, extensive restoration work has been carried out by English Heritage and the castle is today one of the most visited ancient monuments in Britain.

From the magnificent castle grounds, the walker has unsurpassed views of the South and North Bays. Also to be found in the castle grounds are the remains of a Roman signal station.

Return to the castle entrance and continue with St Mary's on the left, into Castle Road. Take the first turning on the right to **Queen's Parade** from where there are wonderful views of Scarborough's North Bay and coastline towards Scalby Mills and Burniston.

Continue to head north past the Clifton Hotel on the left, and the Alexandra Bowls Centre on the right before turning right down the gentle slope of Peasholm Road. Across the road is one of Scarborough's best known holiday attractions, **Peasholm Park**, the setting for the twice weekly Naval Battle – a unique display of warfare which has delighted generations of children since 1927. The smaller of the ten ships are operated by remote control, but each of the larger vessels has a one man crew who has to fire blanks through the gun turrets and keep in contact with the shore and other ships.

Beneath the man-made lake is the Manor of Northstead, one of the two offices of profit under The Crown. When a Member of Parliament wants to resign his seat he applies for the Manor of Northstead, or the Chiltern Hundreds.

Cross the road outside the park to Northstead Manor Gardens and the **North Bay Railway** which runs for just under a mile to Scalby Mills. The locomotives are models of the LNER's Gresley engine but are powered by diesel instead of steam. Each summer the railway carries up to 500,000 passengers.

Walking through **Northstead Manor Gardens**, the long-since

disused Open Air Theatre on the island stage, and its vast 7000 seat auditorium remain as a reminder of the days when crowds travelled from all parts of the North to see the big musical productions of the day.

Continue to head north along the North Bay promenade and with the vast beach on your right, you will reach Scalby Mills, home to the **Sea Life Centre**, one of Scarborough's big holiday success stories of recent years.

Take the road past the Scalby Mills Hotel and into Scalby Mills Road, back to Burniston Road, alongside the seaward side of the North Cliff Golf Course and down to Peasholm Park, returning to the town centre via Columbus Ravine, Northway and Westborough, where at the busy traffic interchange with Valley Bridge Parade, you will find the **Stephen Joseph Theatre**. Here Britain's leading comedy playwright, Sir Alan Ayckbourn, is director of productions.

Sir Alan has become a legend in his own lifetime in Scarborough which he made his home some 40 years ago. He started his career when the late theatre pioneer Stephen Joseph opened his Theatre-in-the-Round in the lecture hall at Scarborough's Central Library in Vernon Road. From there it moved to the converted school hall of the one-time Scarborough High School for Boys, later Westwood School overlooking the Valley Gardens. Here he premiered many of his 50-plus worldwide successes.

The Odeon Cinema had been closed for several years before Sir Alan and his team of the Scarborough Theatre Trust decided to make the brave decision to convert it into a two-theatre complex, one with 450 seats in the highly successful in-the-round design, and the other a traditional end-stage theatre with some 150 seats.

The theatre attracts visitors from around the world and no visit to Scarborough is complete without seeing a production.

Town centre, South Bay and Esplanade

Length of Walk: 3 miles
Start/finish: St Nicholas Cliff

Starting in St Nicholas Cliff, study the architecture of **The Grand Hotel**. Designed by Cuthbert Broderick, famous for other British landmarks including Leeds Town Hall. When it was built, The Grand had a room for every day of the year. In recent years the number has decreased as major modernisation schemes have been carried out to provide en suite bedrooms.

Walk down Falconers Road and cross Vernon Road into **The Crescent**, Scarborough's architectural gem. With the terraces on your right, and the gardens on the left, follow the road to **Woodend Museum**, the home of the literary Sitwell family – Edith, Osbert and Sacheverell. Today it is a natural history museum with a wealth of exhibits depicting life on the Yorkshire Coast including the biggest tunny fish ever caught in the UK.

Next door is the **Scarborough Art Gallery** with a collection which includes works by Atkinson Grimshaw, Turner, and HB Carter, and a regular venue for touring exhibitions.

The Prince of Wales, later Edward VII, often stayed with the Earls of Londesborough at the nearby **Londesborough Lodge**, now the headquarters of the council's Tourism and Leisure Services – until, it is said, he contracted food poisoning which he blamed on Scarborough's sewage system!

Jan A. Ives '09

The Crescent Terraces date back to 1833. Immediately to the south is Belvoir Terrace, named after Belvoir Castle, seat of The Duke of Rutland, the one-time Borough Recorder.

Follow the roadway back to Vernon Road, where on the left is the Central Library and an impressive view of Scarborough as it was in 1735 by John Settrington which suggests that at that time people bathed naked close to the shore in full view of the beach! Although it is difficult to tell the sex of the figures from this distance it would appear that both men and women bathed in this manner until the end of the 18th century.

Turn right and head down the hill towards the sea and Valley Road. On your left is the **Rotunda Museum**, a splendid listed building with an immense collection of Scarborough memorabilia, and well worth a visit.

Cross the roadway, known as Aquarium Top, to the entrance to The Spa. Above you is the **Spa Bridge**, over which some of the greatest politicians of the 20th century have walked en route to The Spa Grand Hall to address conferences.

With the sea wall on your left, the vast **Spa complex** is just 200 yards ahead. It has been the centre of social life in Scarborough for over 300 years and it was here, in 1620, that Elizabeth Farrer noticed that the stones at the bottom of a stream were a distinct russet colour. She re-traced her steps and saw where the stream bubbled from the earth. Tasting the water she found it had an acid taste and probably had medicinal qualities. As a result of her discovery, Scarborough developed a reputation as a place to take the waters and the Spaw, as it became known, soon became the rage with 'persons of quality and the gentry of the country'. Its waters were guaranteed to cure every conceivable ailment!

That was the start of Scarborough as a holiday resort, and even today the waters can still be found trickling through the sea wall in a little niche on steps leading to the beach.

The **Grand Hall**, restored to its original Victorian splendour in the 1980s, is the setting of nightly concerts throughout the summer, while the **Spa**

The Rotunda

20

Theatre's holiday shows are the longest running in any British resort – from mid May until the end of October – and among the most successful at the box office.

The **Ocean Ballroom**, like the Grand Hall, is one of Scarborough's main conference venues by day, and an entertainment centre by night. Nearby is **The Clock Cafe**, an excellent spot to enjoy refreshments and views of the South Bay.

Immediately above the Spa are gardens designed by Joseph Paxton and a steady climb up the winding paths will lead you to

The Esplanade. Alternatively, use the **South Cliff tram lift**, the oldest in the country dating back to 1875, and rising 284ft to The Esplanade and its fine terraced hotels and gardens.

Head back along The Esplanade, and into St Martin's Avenue to the **Church of St Martin's-on-the Hill**, renowned for its paintings by the Pre-Raphaelite painters Rossetti, Burne-Jones and Morris.

Leaving the church, turn left into Albion Road, then right into Ramshill Road. Cross the Valley Bridge, turn right into Somerset Terrace, across the Vernon Road/Falconers Road junction and back to St Nicholas Cliff.

Cliff lift and Grand Hotel

Scalby, Hackness and Raincliffe

Length of Walk: 4 miles
Start/finish: Scalby village

The attractive village of Scalby, which is mentioned in the Domesday Book, has its origins in Scandinavian times, and there is also evidence of a Roman road nearby.

Starting at the centre of the village, outside The Nag's Head public house, walk down High Street towards the picturesque parish church of St Laurence's. Opposite the pub is the Temperance Hall, built on the site of the old village stocks, last used in 1840 to punish drunks!

The first property on the left is **Lancaster Cottage**, a reminder of Scalby's long standing connection with the monarchy and The Duchy of Lancaster which is still a major landowner in the area. In the 13th and 14th centuries it was dominated by forest full of deer, preserved for the King and his friends to hunt.

The fountain nearby was presented to the village to mark the Diamond Jubilee of Queen Victoria in 1897.

St Laurence's church, which has one of the most picturesque settings of any in North Yorkshire, dates back to 1180. One of the pillars in the nave bears the inscription 'Pra Remember the Power'' (Pray remember the poor).

The east window is a fine example of modern stained glass and depicts the life of St Laurence.

The heavy copper weather vane on the tower is said to represent the gridiron on which St Laurence was martyred.

Somewhere in the churchyard is the grave of James Law who, in 1826, was killed in the nearby village of Burniston by a smuggler. Two hand-forged nails driven into one of the buttresses on the north side marks the grave of a local blacksmith, too poor to afford a headstone. Immediately south of the church, overlooking the village green, are **The Church Rooms**, built as a school in 1828 and today used as a social centre for the church.

Across the road leading out of the village is **Low Hall**, a fine red brick mansion built at the turn of the century by the Rowntree family and now a convalescent home for coal miners.

Walking up the long hill of Hay Brow, marvellous views are to be found of the north of Scarborough, before reaching the hamlet of Suffield. From here, head to the village of Hackness through the wooden hillsides with their fine copper beech trees.

On the left is **Hackness Hall**, family seat of Lord and Lady Derwent, built in 1795 by Sir Richard Vanden-Bemp de Johnstone to replace an Elizabethan mansion which stood nearer the lake.

The exterior is a fine example of the later 18th century work of the York School. In 1910, fire destroyed most of the interior but it was restored by Walter Brearley of York. The ballroom is the only room which was restored exactly as it was previously.

Close to The Hall is the parish church of **St Peter** which has close links with Whitby Abbey. It dates from the time of the Northumbrian Kingdom and is believed to have been founded by the Abbey's first Abbess, St Hilda.

The church contains an early 16th century font-cover and repaired stalls with misericords, while in the south aisle are two fragments of pre-conquest cross-shafts, all dating from before the destruction of the parent abbey in 867. These fragments bear the name of Abbess Oedilburga.

Turn left in the village of Hackness, at the village hall, towards

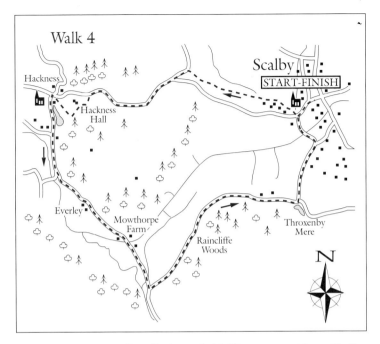

Walk 4

Mowthorpe. You will walk through idyllic countryside, with the River Derwent in the valley below and rolling pastures on each side of the road.

On leaving Mowthorpe, climb the short hill – there's an ideal picnic spot on the right – before turning left into **Raincliffe Woods.** Enjoy the tranquillity of this ancient woodland and its wildlife before reaching **Throxenby Mere** on the right. Take the turning on the left and descend the hill back into Scalby, along Hackness Road on the left, over the stone-built bridge and to the village green.

Walk Five

Cayton Bay, Killerby, and Cayton

Length of walk: 2.5 miles
Start/finish: Cayton Bay

Cayton Bay, some three miles from Scarborough's town centre, has splendid views of the sea and coastline. Using sign-posted Cleveland Way markers, the walker can enjoy excellent scenery and bracing air along the cliff top.

Walk down the cliff path alongside the Beach View Stores to link with the Cleveland Way and admire the cliffs known locally as **Red Cliff Hole** and **Red Cliff Point**, but do not attempt to climb them – they are susceptible to slippage.

The Cleveland Way can be left near Gristhorpe Cliffs and then return to the A165 Scarborough to Filey road which is crossed to the village of hamlet of Killerby and the adjoining village of Cayton.

At Killerby, Valerie Green's **Stained Glass Centre** is well worth a visit in Killerby Lane. Here you can see glass skills dating back in the family business more than a hundred years and an exhibition charts the history of the art from medieval times to the present day. Her work is to be found in many churches throughout Britain. The centre also has an excellent tea-room for its visitors.

On leaving the centre turn left into Cayton village and take the first turning on the right, Mill Lane, which will lead you back to Cayton Bay, past well-landscaped caravan parks and holiday bungalows.

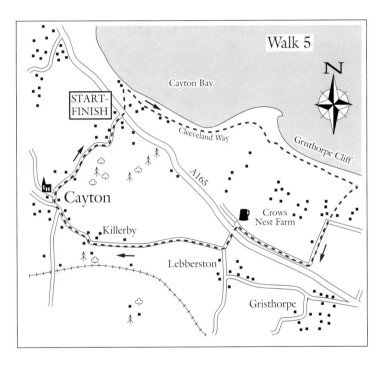

Oliver's Mount and the Mere

Length of walk: 2.5 miles
Start/finish: Queen Margaret's Road and The Mere junction

John A. Ives '00.

The vast area that comprises of The Mere and Oliver's Mount has been designated a country park by the Borough Council following a major restoration of the lake.

Close by is Seamer Valley which was formed during the last Ice Age when ice blocked the Derwent Valley creating a large lake. It overspilled to create a number of valleys, including Seamer Valley and Forge Valley.

The Mere, a lake covering 19 acres is set in attractive landscaped surroundings.

Start your walk at the entrance in Queen Margaret's Road, on the right of the railway bridge. As you walk around the water look out for birds and anglers and during the summer months, model boat enthusiasts and water-skiers.

It was to the island in the centre of the lake that the famous replica of *The Hispaniola* sailed taking generations of holiday-making children before it found a new home in Scarborough Harbour.

You will reach Queen Margaret's road at the end of the Mere walk, and you then turn right into Mere Lane to begin the ascent to **Oliver's Mount**, 500ft above sea level and reputed to be the toughest motor cycle circuit on the British mainland. Races are held two or three times a year but are always well sign-posted so there is no fear of being confronted with a formidable line-up of high-powered machines and their riders.

The original name of the hill was Weaponness, derived from the belief that Oliver Cromwell placed batteries on it during the siege of Scarborough Castle.

There are several routes to walk around the plateau of Oliver's Mount, all of which lead to the Cenotaph and the magnificent views over Scarborough which can be enjoyed from the seats below it. The nearby **Mount Cafe** is open nearly all year. On the right is **Deepdale**, which also has its origins in the Ice Age, and nearby are to be found the remains of a stone quarry which

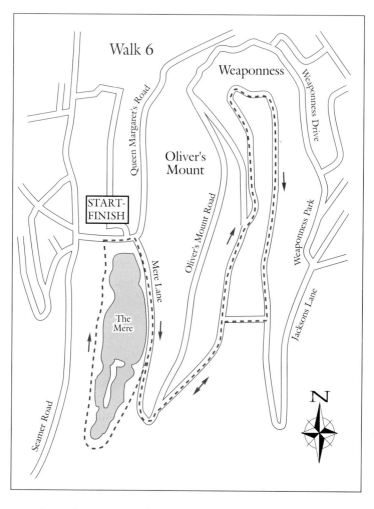

reveals sandstone created some 120 million years ago.

Walk inland from the cenotaph and the road will lead you back to the starting point in Queen Margaret's Road.

OTHER TITLES AVAILABLE FROM DALESMAN

Dalesman Town and City Guide Series
TOWN GUIDE TO HARROGATE Mark Reid   £1.99
TOWN GUIDE TO WHITBY Harry Collett   £1.99
CITY GUIDE TO YORK John Scott   £1.99

Dalesman Pub Walks Series
NORTH YORK MOORS & COAST   Richard Musgrave £5.99

Dalesman Tea Shop Walks Series
NORTH YORK MOORS & COAST Mark Reid £5.99

Walks Around Series
PICKERING Nick Channer £1.99
WHITBY Nick Channer £1.99
KIRKBYMOORSIDE Nick Channer £1.99
HELMSLEY Nick Channer £1.99

Walking Guides
NORTH YORK MOORS Nick Channer £4.99

Available from all good bookshops. In case of difficulty, and for a full list
of Dalesman titles, contact Dalesman Publishing Company, Stable
Courtyard, Broughton Hall, Skipton, North Yorkshire, BD23 3AZ.

Tel: 01756 701381
www.dalesman.co.uk